Keto Diet for Beginners 2020

10 simple keys to Keto Success. Easy and Healthy Everyday Ketogenic Diet Recipes to Reset Your Body and Live a Healthy Life

Jack Masen

© **Copyright 2019 - All rights reserved.**

The content contained within this book may not be reproduced, duplicated or transmitted without direct written permission from the author or the publisher.

Under no circumstances will any blame or legal responsibility be held against the publisher, or author, for any damages, reparation, or monetary loss due to the information contained within this book, either directly or indirectly.

Legal Notice:

This book is copyright protected. It is only for personal use. You cannot amend, distribute, sell, use, quote or paraphrase any part, or the content within this book, without the consent of the author or publisher.

Disclaimer Notice:

Please note the information contained within this document is for educational and entertainment purposes only. All effort has been executed to present accurate, up to date, reliable, complete information. No warranties of any kind are declared or implied. Readers acknowledge that the author is not engaging in the rendering of legal, financial, medical or professional advice. The content within this book has been derived from various sources. Please consult a licensed professional before attempting any techniques outlined in this book.

By reading this document, the reader agrees that under no circumstances is the author responsible for any losses, direct or indirect, that are incurred as a result of the use of the the information contained within this document, including, but not limited to, errors, omissions, or inaccuracies.

Table of Contents

Introduction 6
10. Keys for Keto Success 8
   1. Observe Keto Diet Proportions. 8
   2. Reduce the Amount of Protein Ingested. 10
   3. Add Good Fats. 11
   4. Optimize Your Carbohydrates 14
   5. Drink More Water. 16
   6. Watch the Ceonsumption of Sufficient Amounts of Minerals and Vitamins. 17
   7. Add Physical Exercise into your Life. 18
   8. Relieve Stress Through Meditation. 21
   9. A Good Dream is the key to Success. 22
   10. Four Quick Ways to Return to Ketosis. 24
Chapter 1 – Breakfast Recipes 26
   1. Omelet with Mushrooms and Goat Cheese 26
   2. Cheese Keto Rolls with Cauliflower 28
   3. Bulletproof Coffee 31
   4. Cabbage Cheese Sandwiches 33
   5. Perfect Keto Pancakes 35
   6. Vegetarian Keto Porridge 37
   7. Keto French Pancakes 39
   8. Seafood Omelet 41
   9. Vegetable Casserole 43
   10. Stuffed Gourmet Avocado 45
   11. Low-Carb Sour Berry Cake 47
   12. Stuffed Avocado 49
Chapter 2 – Lunch Keto Recipes 51

1. Tonic Keto Soup with Egg 51
2. Chicken Cream Soup 53
3. Creamy Turnip Puree 55
4. Spinach Cream Soup 57
5. Chicken Soup with Cabbage 59
6. Beef Croquettes with Cheese 61
7. Cauliflower and Cheese Casserole 63
8. Keto Steak with Vegetables and Spices 65
9. Zucchini Noodle Shrimp 67
10. Baked Cauliflower with Cheese 69

Chapter 3 – Dinner 71

1. Rissole in Bacon 71
2. Stuffed Chicken Peppers 73
3. Egg Keto Salad with Avocado 75
4. Baked Eggs with Ham and Asparagus 77
5. Egg Keto Pizza 79
6. Egg Rolls 81
7. Chicken Cutlets 83
8. Chicken Rolls with Parmesan 85
9. Turkey and Spinach Meatballs 87
10. Baked Chicken Fillet with Cheese 89
11. Turkey Rolls 91

Chapter 4 - Fish Recipes 93

1. Monkfish Rolls with Ham 93
2. Salmon Cutlets with Fresh Herbs 95
3. Salmon or Trout with Cream Sauce 97
4. Baked Shrimp with Garlic and Butter 99
5. Salmon Fruits with Sauce 101

    6. Fried Salmon with Parmesan 103

    7. Salmon with Seasoning 105

Chapter 5 - Snacks / Salads 108

    1. Cheese Keto Chips 108

    2. Spicy Eggs 110

    3. Eggs with Spices 112

    4. Egg Keto-Cupcakes 114

    5. Kale Chips 116

    6. Peanut Butter Cookie 118

    7. Cheesy Cauliflower Croquettes 120

Chapter 6: Ketogenic Sauces 122

    1. Keto Parmesan Pesto 122

    2. Salsa Sauce 124

    3. Blue Cheese Sauce 126

    4. Thai Peanut Sauce 128

    5. Avocado & Yogurt Sauce with Salad Cilantro .. 130

Chapter 7 – Keto Approved Desserts 132

    1. Chocolate Pancakes 132

    2. Chocolate Brownie in a Mug 134

    3. Chocolate Truffles 136

    4. Chia Pudding 138

    5. Chocolate Keto Cake with Blueberry 140

    6. Chocolate Mousse 143

    7. Delicious Brownies 145

    8. Coconut Raspberry Cake 147

    9. Ice Cream with Avocado 150

Conclusion 152

Introduction

Many are set to become slimmer. These are the realities of our lives. But you want not only to lose weight, but also do no harm to your health. Unfortunately, not all diets are equally beneficial . But some will help you not only lose weight, but also improve your health.

If you need a truly effective and safe method, then pay attention to the Ketogenic Diet or Keto Diet, as it is often called. In a nutshell, a ketogenic or Keto Diet is a high-fat diet. But it would be wrong to think that only in this is the whole point of the Keto Diet. In fact, in a Keto Diet, the correct ratio of all nutrients is essential. Thus, there should be a lot of fat from which the body consumes energy, a moderate amount of proteins, and minimal carbohydrates. In percentage terms, this means that fat should be 70%, proteins 25%, and carbohydrates 5%. When the body receives nutrients in this ratio, it enters a metabolic state known as ketosis. This is a reasonable physiological condition that provides the ability to get energy from fats. Not to be confused with ketoacidosis. The latter is a pathological condition and can occur, as a rule, in people with diabetes.

So, ketosis is a desired condition for the body, in which its metabolism changes and switches to the use of fats as fuel. This is just one of the tools that are available for metabolism control.

Therefore, you can forget the classically held beliefs that fat makes you fat. This is only true if in addition to fat, you consume large amounts of carbohydrates. And one can hardly assume that the constant "swing" of the transition from one type of metabolism to another allows the body to "relax." A Keto Diet is instead not a diet, but a healthy lifestyle.

10. Keys for Keto Success

How easy it is to get into ketosis and follow a Keto Diet!

So that the process of losing weight and improving health is fast and effective, we have prepared 10 keys for you and recommend reading them in this section. They will help you understand the basic principles of the Keto Diet, and get key recommendations for easy passing keto diet

1. Observe Keto Diet Proportions.

The ketosis formula looks like this:
Proteins - 20% Fat - 75% Carbohydrates - 5%

If you strictly adhere to these proportions, then your body is in constant ketosis, that is, it takes energy not from glucose derived from carbohydrates, but from ketones synthesized from fat.

To track your macros, it is convenient to use applications or any keto calculators.

Ketone diet prohibits eating not only bread, flour and pasta, pastry, sweets, any sweets, sweet juices and soda, but also any fast carbohydrates, almost all fruits, and vegetables with a high starch content (especially potatoes, corn and peas) and most cereals - from semolina, bulgur and couscous (all this is wheat), ending with oatmeal.

2. Reduce the Amount of Protein Ingested.

Feature ketogenic (keto) diets from another low-carb ration is that it contains a moderate amount of protein does not constitute a significant part of the diet, unlike fat. Cause-with an excess of protein, the body can convert it into glucose (gluconeogenesis), so if you sort out a protein, the body's transition into. The state of "ketosis" is much more complicated. This is especially important during the initial stages of the diet.

Protein intake should be:
• If you have a sedentary lifestyle, from 0.6 to 0.8 g of protein per pound of body weight is recommended.
• If you are active, 0.8 to 1.0 g of protein per pound of body weight is recommended.
• If you are exercising with a weight, it is recommended from 1.0 g to 1.2 g of protein per pound of body weight.
Experiment with these ranges to find the right amount of protein. If you do not consume enough protein, your body will not support muscle mass. If you eat too much protein, you will struggle to get into ketosis.

3. Add Good Fats.

Everyone knows that the keto-diet requires increased fat intake, but it is not always clear how this can be done. In the beginning, it can perplex ordinary people who are not used to fatty foods. Do not be afraid, do not starve. You need to properly add healthy fats in your diet. How to do it?

- ✓ Start with the consumption of whole foods and remove all skim from the diet! This is a good start. Remove from the refrigerator and never buy products with the "fat free" icon. Only full-fat cream, cottage cheese, natural yogurt, cheeses. If you go for the meat - only fatty pieces, no lean meat. Add more fatty fish to your diet, likewise cod liver too.

- ✓ Cook on fats. Stop trying to fry the patties on the water in a non-stick pan. Say "NO" to dry chicken breasts! Cook on fats, fry meat, fish, eggs on the right natural fats.
- ✓ Use different fats for a variety of tastes. Fats can greatly change the taste of your dish. For example, beef steak has a completely different taste, if you fry it not just on coconut oil, but on lard, and at the end add butter.
- ✓ Fill all dishes and salads with oil. There are lots of options for sauces and dressings, not only for salads, based on good fats with a minimum amount of carbohydrates, you will find recipes below.
- ✓ Add fatty foods to your diet. Do not hesitate - fatty meat, fatty fish, cheese, avocados, olives, nuts, in all there is not just fat, but a lot of valuable vitamins and minerals. All this can be easily added to almost any dish.
- ✓ Add fat to coffee and tea. No coffee cream in small packages! Only 33% cream without stabilizers! You can add butter or coconut oil. Over time, this can replace breakfast without feeling hungry or kill hunger between meals.
- ✓ Add fatty snacks to your diet. Yes, snacking is generally undesirable on a keto diet, but for the first

time it is very important to teach your body to eat and be saturated with fatty healthy food. Different snacking options that help avoid hunger can help a lot. It is better to eat something than to starve. There are lots of options and recipes - cheese, boiled eggs, nuts, seeds, flax bread, etc.

4. Optimize Your Carbohydrates

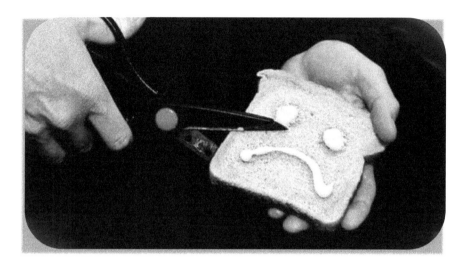

Of course, all people have different organisms and a single approach, of course not, but you can follow the following recommendations:

• It is best to avoid carbohydrates in the morning and choose MCT (middle-chain triglicerides) keto-coffee instead, or a protein-rich breakfast instead.

• As for carbs for the rest of your day or evening, it depends on what you are going to do with them. Most people have enough fat to use as energy when they are in ketosis and perform light and moderate exercises.

Remove simple carbohydrates from the diet.

Always choose glucose, not fructose. Fructose replenishes glycogen stores in the liver, not in the muscles. Because of this, fructose will inhibit ketosis, while glucose will immediately go to work.

You should eat healthy, complex carbohydrates, but at the same time watch your macros and the glycemic index of foods.

Thus, the best carbohydrates include:

- Asparagus
- Artichokes
- Broccoli
- Cauliflower
- Sweet potato
- Zucchini
- Brussels sprouts
- Leafy greens such as spinach and kale
- Nuts (almonds, macadamia, Brazilian and walnuts)
- Raspberry and blackberry
- Chia and flax seeds

When you finally reach ketosis, you should have enough energy so that you can train with a very small amount of carbohydrates from your diet.

But if you do not have enough fast carbohydrates, you should try using MCT oil, as it is an easily accessible source of energy. The MCT is easily digested, so you can use it without worrying about your sudden recovery.

5. Drink More Water.

You can't go wrong with water, especially on a ketogenic diet. During the first few days of carbohydrate restriction, the body usually loses water and minerals at double speed. After a couple of days - when the ketone levels increase - more water will be removed from the body.

To counteract dehydration, which can cause carbohydrate restriction, daily water intake is 2 to 2.5 liters per day for girls and 3-4 liters for men. If you drink an insufficient amount of water, you may get bad breath and urine. (You can add a little lemon or salt). Water helps the work of the kidneys, which at first will process the excess liquid, which in turn was kept by those carbohydrates.

6. Watch the Consumption of Sufficient Amounts of Minerals and Vitamins.

When an organism goes into ketosis, all glycogen stores are burned along with which a lot of water is lost, which leads to an imbalance of the mineral balance. Therefore, on the keto diet, especially at the beginning of it, one should be especially careful to ensure sufficient intake of magnesium, potassium and sodium. This can be done either with food supplements or with a balanced diet.

Without carbohydrate products containing potassium and magnesium in large quantities: hemp seeds, pumpkins, flax, sunflower; almond, Brazilian nuts, pine nuts, spinach, seaweed, avocado.

Due to the decrease in insulin during the Keto Diet, you will quickly lose sodium and potassium. It can cause fatigue, headaches, constipation and cramps. Be sure to pre-stock up with a multi-vitamin complex and separately with calcium, magnesium, potassium and sodium - these guys will always be needed. With sodium everything is clear - do not forget to salt the food. At the end of the book, we will share our shopping cart for these supplements.

7. Add Physical Exercise into your Life.

A light cardio will help reduce cortisol levels, calm down insulin and help distract from bad thoughts about sweets. Everything will come time and jogging, and strength training, and favorite group classes, but later. While you are adapting to ketosis, do not rape your body with a lot of exercise. Additional stress can throw you out of ketosis.

When you are already adapting to a keto diet, your body will be able to accumulate muscle glycogen - a form of glucose accumulation - which is then wasted during intense exercise. But while you are in the process of keto adaptation and are not quite ready to fully use ketones as energy, lighter exercises will suit you.

In the morning, do exercises with low intensity.

When you wake up, fill the bottle with water and a pinch of salt, and go for a walk. The walk should be at a pace where you can easily talk without gasping. It is desirable to walk about an hour.

As you continue walking, you should feel better and better and more and more awake. This is a form of low intensity exercise that will help increase fat burning, and you will not have to suffer from keto flu.

Top 3 physical exercises for keto novices

1. Easy cardio

Some aerobic exercises are great for beginners on a ketogenic diet, but with the proviso that their intensity is quite low (40-50% of your maximum heart rate).

During the transition to ketosis, choose the following cardiovascular exercises:

- Hiking
- Swimming
- Bicycle riding
- Rowing

2. Training with low weight

On keto, contrary to conventional wisdom, you do not need carbohydrates to build muscle.

Regardless of whether you are fully adapted to keto or not, eating enough protein and the presence of ketones in the blood helps maintain muscle mass and increase strength. Therefore, classes with low weight are quite suitable for beginners.

3. Flexibility exercises

Keto yoga you need to include flexibility exercises in your workout program to prevent various injuries and improve coordination. For example:
- Yoga
- Pilates
- Gymnastics

8. Relieve Stress Through Meditation.

When you start a ketogenic diet, you may be tenser and more irritable than usual. This is due to the fact that your cortisol levels are slightly higher than usual.

To help reduce cortisol and improve overall well-being, it is best to do daily meditation.

Every day for 15 minutes, just sit silently, inhaling and exhaling slowly and deeply. If you have a thought or desire to do something, turn your attention to your breathing. This is meditation in its simplest form.

The purpose of meditation is not to be thoughtless, so as not to be distracted by the thought, but to concentrate on breathing. This is how you train your mind so that life is less stressful.

9. A Good Dream is the key to Success.

Another way to reduce stress is to ensure good sleep. Good sleep is especially important for ketogenic diets. Without this, cortisol levels will increase, which complicates keto-flu and keto-adaptation.

Sleep for at least 7-9 hours every night, and if you feel tired in the middle of the day, lie down for 30 minutes or meditate.

To fall asleep faster at night, turn off all light sources (including the phone) at least 30 minutes before you go to bed. This will help you translate your mind from work mode to sleep mode.

Try not to eat anything within four hours of bedtime. This gives you plenty of time to recycle energy from the last meal, as well as provide enough fuel so that you don't wake up hungry in the middle of the night.

The room where you will sleep should be cool and dark, but your limbs should be warm. Researchers have noticed that when your arms and legs are warmer than the surrounding air, your body speeds up the process of falling asleep.

Do not exercise before bedtime.

Drink coffee only in the morning.

10. Four Quick Ways to Return to Ketosis.

The situation described in this article is more than typical. You interrupted the state of ketosis while on a trip or staged yourself a day when you can eat everything- it is not so important what it was. We will look at the four fastest ways to return to the state of ketosis.

The first way. Include in your next workout in the exercise room and on the upper body and lower. I know that you usually do not do that, but now it's worth it.

Alternating exercises to the top and bottom of the body, we more effectively move our lymph

The lymphatic system is completely separate from the circulatory system, a network of vessels running throughout the body. Basically, it carries white blood cells, some proteins, and very few red blood cells. The main task is to supply the body with essential substances and vice versa, to remove toxins. What does this have to do with ketosis? Lymph transports fatty acids. In fact, fats travel through the lymphatic system even before they enter the circulatory system. In contrast to the blood that the heart drives through the vessels, the lymph moves through the lymphatic vessels only due to the reduction of skeletal muscles and that is why we need to do exercises on different parts of the body in one workout. This will get into the liver, converting to ketones and returning us to ketosis faster.

The second way. Caffeine. Increasing the caffeine dose during this period is guaranteed to increase the number of ketones produced. However, it is still necessary to exercise caution and moderation, using this method to return to ketosis and not to go through a dose of caffeine.

The third way. MCT oil. Why is it worth to double your usual dose of MCT oil for a speedy return to ketosis? Because this oil does not have to pass through the liver to participate in the ketone production process. Usually, they consume fat through the entire path and then get into the liver. MCT oil from the digestive system is immediately sent to the bloodstream, bypassing the liver, and is instantly used in mitochondria.

The fourth way. It is unlikely to suit beginners - fasting. In the process of fasting, your body produces the hormone glucagon, which causes the body to utilize all the glycogen to the maximum. So, glycogen is used and the body starts to produce ketones accelerated. It must be admitted that in this case the muscles will be partially split to obtain nutrients, but in small quantities.

All of the above methods will help you to quickly return to ketosis and the first three of them can be used by beginners for the initial entry into it.

Chapter 1 – Breakfast Recipes

1. Omelet with Mushrooms and Goat Cheese

Omelet - one of the most popular breakfast items. It is not surprising, because the Directions of an omelet take a minimum of time. It is quite nourishing for a morning meal and very tasty. To make an omelet with mushrooms and cheese, you will need a little more time than the Directions of a classic omelet, but the result is worth it. You will love this lush, porous, juicy and very tasty omelet.

Servings: 2
Prep Time: 5 minutes
Cook Time: 10 minutes

Ingredients:
- 3 large eggs
- 2 tsp. of heavy cream
- 85 g of chopped mushrooms
- 1 tsp. of olive oil
- 56 g of crumbled goat cheese
- Seasoning to taste
- Green onions for garnish

Directions:
1. Brown the mushrooms in olive oil for about 4 minutes.
2. While the above mushroom preparation is going on, beat the eggs with heavy cream and seasonings.
3. Pour the egg mixture over the mushrooms and cook for about 2-3 minutes.
4. Add goat cheese. Fold the omelet in half and continue as "3" above until the cheese starts to melt.
5. Serve with spring onions or with another side dish according to your taste.

Nutrients per serving:
- Calories: 268 kcal
- Fat: 22g
- Carbs: 1.14g
- Protein: 20.54g

2. Cheese Keto Rolls with Cauliflower

Cheese keto rolls are just perfect as a snack. They can also be eaten for breakfast. They are simply irreplaceable if you need it suddenly or urgently in 20-30 minutes, and you need to create something tasty and not very complicated. Greens any suit: dill, parsley, basil - whatever you like!

Servings: 3
Prep Time: 5 minutes
Cook Time: 30 minutes

Ingredients:

- 90 g of cauliflower
- 4 eggs, separate whites, and yolks

- 1 clove of garlic, crushed
- 2 pieces of melted cheese, rub on a grater
- 50 g of hard cheese, grated
- 50 g of homemade mayonnaise
- salt to taste
- black pepper to taste
- 1 bunch of greens, chopped finely

Directions:

1. Blanch the color cabbage for 5 minutes.
2. Grind cauliflower.
3. Heat the oven to 350 F degrees.
4. Beat squirrels into lush foam and for the time being left behind.
5. Mix the cauliflower with the yolks, and then gently mix in the whipped whites.
6. Put the mixture on the whole baking sheet and smooth with a spatula; put in the oven for 15 minutes.
7. For the filling, mix whole grated cheese with garlic, spices, salt, greens, and homemade mayonnaise.
8. Carefully put the base for the roll on the food film.
9. On the base, lay the filling and level up with a spatula.
10. Wrap the roll carefully. Cut the roll into portions and put them on the plate

Nutrients per serving:

- Carbs: 1.06 g
- Fat: 6.58 g
- Protein: 5.14 g
- Calories: 74 kcal

3. Bulletproof Coffee

In taste, this drink is like a creamy latte but does not contain sugar or milk. As for the effect, it does not only invigorates and improves cognitive functions, it also helps to improve metabolism and reduce cholesterol.

Servings: 1
Prep Time: 5 minutes
Cook Time: 10 minutes

Ingredients:

- 1 cup of water

- 2 tbsp. of coffee
- 1 tbsp. of grass fed butter
- 1 tbsp. of coconut oil
- ¼ tsp. of vanilla extract

Directions:

1. Make coffee to your taste.
2. Add the coffee, butter and coconut oil to the blender.
3. Add the vanilla extract and a pinch of cinnamon; blend for 20 seconds.

Nutrients per serving:

- Calories: 284 kcal
- Fat: 24.43g
- Carbs: 0.14g
- Protein: 16.54g

4. Cabbage Cheese Sandwiches

I offer original cheese cauliflower sandwiches.

Servings: 2
Prep Time: 5 min
Cook Time: 30min

Ingredients:

- 400 g of "rice" from cauliflower
- 1 tsp. of salt (optional)
- 1 tbsp. of dried parsley
- 1/2 cup of Parmesan cheese
- 1 egg
- 4 slices of cheddar cheese

Directions:

1. Cook the rice from cauliflower in the microwave for about

6 minutes.
2. Add salt, Parmesan cheese, dried parsley, and egg. Mix everything well.
3. Put the mixture in the baking dish. Divide it into squares, according to the type of toast.
4. Bake each side for about 15 minutes.
5. Put one piece of cabbage bread into the pan; stuffing on top (I used cheddar cheese), and cover it with a second loaf.
6. Cover the pan with a lid and cook for about 5 minutes on each side.

Nutrients per serving:

- Calories: 382 kcal
- Fat: 24.1 g
- Carbs: 5.2 g
- Protein: 30.5 g

5. Perfect Keto Pancakes

Quick and tasty! Pancakes are very tender and soft.

Servings: 4
Prep Time: 5 minutes
Cook Time: 15 minutes

Ingredients:

- 4 tsps. of maple extract
- 60 g of almond flour
- 8 eggs
- 4 tsp. Of cinnamon
- 8 tablespoons of coconut oil
- 2 ¾ oz. pork rinds

Directions:

1. Grind pork rinds in a blender. Then add everything to the rest of the ingredients and mix them until smooth.
2. Heat a skillet to medium (300-400°F) and add the coconut oil into it.
3. Pour batter into the skillet, fry it until golden brown (around 2 minutes), and of course, don't forget to flip it!
4. Bonus: If you want a sweet finish, you can add some fruit (for example strawberries) to it.

Nutrients per serving:

- Calories: 510 kcal
- Fat: 43 g
- Carbs: 2 g
- Protein: 24 g

6. Vegetarian Keto Porridge

Sometimes you can get bored with ordinary human porridge on a keto diet, if you have loved them before. Yes, porridge is convenient and fast; it is tasty and beautiful. Porridge can also be a full-fledged breakfast, lunch or just a dessert. You can eat it and enjoy life, or drink a delicious bronkofe. It all depends on the composition and your needs.

Servings: 1
Prep Time: 5 minutes
Cook Time: 10minutes

Ingredients:
- 2 tablespoons of coconut flour
- 3 tablespoons of golden flax flour

- 2 tablespoons of vegetarian vanilla protein powder
- 1 ½ cup of unsweetened almond milk
- Erythritol powder to taste

Directions:

1. Mix in a bowl coconut flour, golden flax flour, and protein powder.
2. Add almond milk and cook over medium heat.
3. When the porridge begins to thicken, you can add a sugar substitute to your taste - for example, ½ tablespoon.
4. Serve with your favorite supplements (berries, etc.).

Nutrients per serving:

- Calories: 249 kcal
- Fat: 13.07 g
- Carbs: 5.78 g
- Protein: 17.82 g

7. Keto French Pancakes

According to this recipe, pancakes are thin and delicate like velvet. Preparing velvet pancakes on eggs and cream.

Servings: 4
Prep Time: 5 minutes
Cook Time: 15 minutes

Ingredients:
- 8 eggs
- 2 cups of whipping cream
- ¼ tsp. of Salt
- ½ cup of Water
- 3 oz. of Butter
- 2 tbsp. of husk psyllium powder, ground

Directions:
1. Combine the salt, water, cream, and eggs in a medium bowl. Mix using a hand mixer.
2. Now add the ground husk gradually while whisking. Continue to mix until the texture become very smooth. Let the mixture rest for about 10 minutes.
3. One pancake with ½ cup of batter. Fry on medium heat in butter, same as regular pancakes.
4. Don't rush, let the top becomes almost dry and then flip it.
5. Enjoy!

Tip!
Many things can affect the batter; like for example, the egg slice, the quality of the psyllium husk, the cream, etc. So, the first pancake that you fry should be a test. See how it goes and accordingly, add more powder or water.

Serve these delicious pancakes with berries and whipped cream or anything you like, but stick to keto.

Nutrients per serving:
- Calories: 682 kcal
- Fat: 68 g
- Carbs: 4 g
- Protein: 16 g

8. Seafood Omelet

So, you love Seafood? An omelet is undoubtedly the best option for breakfast, and adding seafood to it makes it very tasty and unique.

Servings: 4
Prep Time: 5 minutes
Cook Time: 15 minutes

Ingredients:
- 12 eggs
- 4 garlic cloves
- 1 cup of mayonnaise (of course you can lower it according to your taste)

- 2 red chili peppers
- 10 oz. Of boiled shrimp or some seafood mix
- 4 tbsp. Of olive oil
- chives
- 4 tbs. of olive oil/butter
- salt and pepper to your taste

Directions:
1. Heat the frying pan, and fry seafood, garlic, and chili in olive oil; add salt and pepper to taste. Then set it aside and cool to room temperature.
2. Add the chives (optional) and mayo to the cooled mixture.
3. Whisk the eggs together, season them, and fry them in a skillet.
4. Add the mix. When your omelet is almost ready, fold it, lower the temperature a bit, and let it set completely. Serve it immediately for the best taste.

Nutrients per serving:
- Calories: 872 kcal
- Fat: 83 g
- Carbs: 4 g
- Protein: 27 g

9. Vegetable Casserole

This dish turns out very tasty and tender; bright, and satisfying. Try to make a casserole from this recipe, and I am sure that it will surprise you with its excellent taste.

Servings: 3
Prep Time: 10 minutes
Cook Time: 30 minutes

Ingredients:
- 8 oz. of shredded mozzarella cheese
- 8 oz. of shredded cheddar cheese
- 6 large eggs
- 1 cup of cauliflower
- 4 tbsps. of butter

Directions:

1. Carefully mix the cheeses and eggs.
2. Butter the bottom of a skillet; add the cauliflower and the cheese mixture. Set oven to 350F, and bake for 35 minutes; then for 30 more minutes at 250 degrees F.
3. Serve

Nutrients per serving:

- Calories: 782kcal
- Fats: 62.6g
- Carbs: 4.4g
- Protein: 51.6g

10. Stuffed Gourmet Avocado

This recipe is made for those days when the morning is heavy, you are late, and you need to cook something quickly!

Servings: 1
Prep Time: 5 minutes
Cook Time: 15 minutes

Ingredients:

- 1 ripe avocado
- salt
- 1 lemon (the juice part of it)
- 1 oz. of goat cheese
- 2 ozs. of smoked salmon

Directions:

1. Cut the avocado, and remove the seed.
2. Mix the remaining ingredients, until they fuse well.
3. Place the cream inside the avocado.

Tip: If you want small snacks, you can cut the avocado into small pieces and serve it that way.

Nutrients per serving:

- Calories: 471 kcal
- Fat: 41 g
- Carbs: 4 g
- Protein: 19 g

11. Low-Carb Sour Berry Cake

This original, delicious breakfast can satisfy you all morning. The cupcakes are the perfect way to energize your day.

Serves: 15
Prep Time: 15 minutes
Cook Time: 20 minutes

Ingredients:
- 2 cups of almond flour
- ½ tsp. of baking soda
- ¼ cup of Erythritol
- 1 cup of sour cream

- ½ tsp. of salt
- 2 eggs
- 4 ounces of blueberries, fresh
- 1/8 cup of butter, melted

Directions:
1. In the preheated oven 350 ° F, Place cupcake papers inside the individual muffin holes of your muffin tin.
2. Next, mix all the dry ingredients.
3. In another bowl, beat the eggs lightly. Add the butter and sour cream. Mix until thoroughly combined.
4. Combine the almond flour mixture with the sour cream mixture. Stir until thoroughly mixed. Add the blueberries until they are evenly incorporated.
5. Pour the resulting dough into forms paper up to ½ full.
6. Bake the muffins until golden, or for about 20 minutes.

Allow to slightly cool. Serve hot with butter.

Nutrients per serving:
- Calories: 147 kcal
- Fat: 13 g
- Carbs: 5 g
- Protein: 5 g

12. Stuffed Avocado

Stuffed avocado with bacon has an unusually delicate flavor and is among the exquisite dishes. This recipe will satisfy you for a long time.

Servings: 2
Prep Time: 5 minutes
Cook Time: 30minutes

Ingredients:
- 1 avocado, pitted and cut in half
- 1 tbsp. of salted butter
- 3 large eggs
- 3 slices of bacon, cut into small pieces
- A pinch of salt and black pepper

Directions:

1. Clean out most of the avocado pulp, leaving about 1.5 cm around.
2. Place a large frying pan over low heat and add butter, to warm up. Beat and mix the eggs thoroughly in a bowl, adding a pinch of salt and pepper.
3. Place bacon on one side of the pan and fry for a couple of minutes. On the other side, pour the egg mixture and stir them regularly.
4. Eggs and bacon should be prepared 5 minutes after adding eggs to the pan. If you find that the eggs are cooked a little before the bacon, remove the scrambled eggs and place them in a bowl.
5. Mix the bacon and scrambled eggs together, and then fill the avocado halves with the mixture.

Nutrients per serving:

- Calories: 300 kcal
- Fat: 44 g
- Carbs: 5 g
- Protein: 25 g

Chapter 2 – Lunch Keto Recipes

1. Tonic Keto Soup with Egg

This soup recipe is quite unusual, as coconut chips are added to the bone broth. And then beaten eggs are added to the broth. Soup with very good tones!

Servings: 2
Prep Time: 5 minutes
Cook Time: 30minutes

Ingredients:

- 1 liter of bone broth
- 1 tbsp. of coconut shavings
- 1 tbsp. of sesame oil

- 4 large eggs
- Green onions
- Cilantro
- salt spices to taste

Directions:

1. Mix broth with coconut and sesame oil.
2. Beat the eggs and slowly pour them into the boiling broth in a thin stream, gently stirring the broth.
3. Immediately, serve garnished with green onions, cilantro and plenty of sesame oil.

Nutrients per serving:

- Calories: 259 kcal
- Fat: 17 g
- Carbs: 4 g
- Protein: 23 g

2. Chicken Cream Soup

Delicate and very tasty pumpkin and zucchini puree soup. Preparing chicken soup in chicken broth is quick and easy.

Servings: 4
Prep Time: 5 minutes
Cook Time: 30minutes

Ingredients:

- 1.5 liter of chicken broth
- 400g of chicken, cooked and shredded
- 3 1/2 cups of fresh pumpkin in cubes
- 1 lime juice fruit

- 2 medium zucchini
- 1 cup of coconut cream
- Black pepper, salt, herbs to taste

Directions:

1. Add the pumpkin and zucchini in a pot and simmer on low heat for about 15 minutes.
2. Grind with a blender.
3. Add lime juice, coconut cream, sliced chicken and spices.
4. Serve hot with greens

Nutrients per serving:

- Calories: 170 kcal
- Fat: 14 g
- Carbs: 5 g
- Protein: 15 g

3. Creamy Turnip Puree

Hearty thick puree, with a delicate flavor and a pleasant aroma.

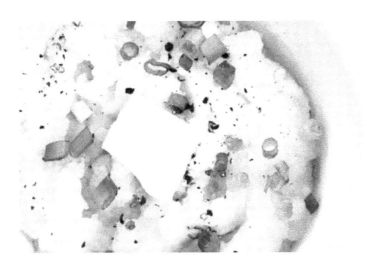

Servings: 3
Prep Time: 5 minutes
Cook Time: 20minutes

Ingredients

- 4 large turnips
- 2 tbsp. of butter or ghee
- Pinch of Himalayan Pink Salt

Directions:

1. Turnip cut into cubes. Boil in water for about 10-15

minutes.
2. Take a fork and soften the vegetables until the mixture looks like mashed potatoes.
3. Add oil and pink salt.

Nutrients per serving:
- Calories: 88 kcal
- Fat: 13 g
- Carbs: 4 g
- Protein: 1.3 g

4. Spinach Cream Soup

Spinach cream soup - tender, light, very tasty, and will undoubtedly please fans of vegetable soups. It has a pleasant texture and delicate taste. Like all cream soups, it is well saturated but leaves a feeling of lightness. Nutmeg and garlic add spice to the dish.

Servings: 4
Prep Time: 5 minutes
Cook Time: 30minutes

Ingredients:
- 280 g of fresh chopped spinach
- 1 cup of heavy cream

- 4 cups of chicken broth
- 1/3 cup of grated parmesan
- 1 tbsp. of butter
- 2 cloves of minced garlic
- 1/4 tsp. of nutmeg
- Salt and pepper to taste
- 4 slices of bacon

Directions:
1. In a saucepan, sauté spinach in butter. Pour in chicken broth and simmer for 5 minutes.
2. Meanwhile, brown the crisp bacon, and then slice into small pieces.
3. Beat the soup with a blender.
4. Put the pan back on the fire, add heavy cream and parmesan, and boil. Mix with nutmeg, salt, and pepper.
5. When serving, garnish with chopped bacon and parmesan (optional).

Nutrients per serving:
- Calories: 395 kcal
- Fat: 36.3 g
- Carbs: 3.8 g
- Protein: 14.4 g

5. Chicken Soup with Cabbage

Chicken soup with cabbage is a great solution for a hearty lunch. To prepare such a dish is simple; you will need ordinary foods, and less than an hour of time. Chicken soup turns out rich, fragrant and very tasty.

Servings: 3
Prep Time: 5 minutes
Cook Time: 30minutes

Ingredients:

- 2 tbsp. of coconut oil
- ½ medium size cubed shallot

- 226 g of chicken thighs
- 2 cups of cauliflower "rice"
- 4 cups of chicken broth
- Pepper and salt to taste

Directions:

1. Fry onion together with chicken thighs, cauliflower rice, and coconut oil.
2. Cook until everything is slightly browned.
3. Add the broth and bring to a boil.
4. Then reduce the heat, and add salt and black pepper.
5. Cook for 25 minutes and serve.

Nutrients per serving:

- Calories: 312 kcal
- Fat: 45 g
- Carbs: 6 g
- Protein: 28.6 g

6. Beef Croquettes with Cheese

A very simple and easy recipe for delicious meatballs. Delicate, juicy meatballs will offer you for lunch.

Servings: 4
Prep Time: 5 minutes
Cook Time: 30 minutes

Ingredients:

- 500g of minced beef
- 1 piece of sausage
- 1 cup of cheddar cheese
- 1/3 cup of shredded pork skins

- 2 large eggs
- Salt, and pepper to taste

Directions:

1. Mix everything together until you can form the meatballs.
2. Place them on a baking sheet with baking sheet.
3. Bake in the oven for 30 minutes at 350 ° F.
4. Add tomato sauce if desired.

Nutrients per serving:

- Calories: 530 kcal
- Fat: 49 g
- Carbs: 0.3 g
- Protein: 41.25 g

7. Cauliflower and Cheese Casserole

Cauliflower casserole turns out tender, juicy, with a soft creamy flavor. This recipe does not require expensive products, and the taste of the dish turns out just fabulous.

Servings: 5
Prep Time: 5 minutes
Cook Time: 30 minutes

Ingredients:

- 1 medium cauliflower
- ½ medium size onion

- 1 cup of sour cream
- 1 cup of crushed cheddar cheese
- Salt and pepper to taste

Directions:

1. Slice the cauliflower, cut the onion into slices, and place them in a baking dish.
2. Add cheese and sour cream to the dish, and mix everything together.
3. Bake at 350 ° F for 20 minutes.

Nutrients per serving:

- Calories: 245 kcal
- Fat: 20.48 g
- Carbs: 4 g
- Protein: 21 g

8. Keto Steak with Vegetables and Spices

A simple dish for lunch. Directions on steak with vegetables. Both pork and beef will do. You can season the steak with garlic.

Servings: 4
Prep Time: 5 minutes
Cook Time: 20minutes

Ingredients:

- 456 g of steak (sliced into strips)
- 2 red bell peppers
- 1 bow
- 2 cloves of garlic
- 1/4 cup of lime juice

- salt, pepper, and herbs to taste

Directions:

1. Fry the steak on each side for 3-5 minutes in olive oil.
2. Fry onions and bell peppers for 2-3 minutes.
3. Add the meat back onto the vegetables inside the pan, and add the spices and garlic.
4. Cook for 10mins.
5. Remove the meat from the heat and pour it with lime juice. 6. Serve with greens.

Nutrients per serving:

- Calories: 226 kcal
- Fat: 18 g
- Carbs: 5 g
- Protein: 21 g

9. Zucchini Noodle Shrimp

An original and tasty dish that can be prepared not only for lunch but also for dinner. Easy and quick to cook, it has an unusual taste ... this dish will surely be pleasant to you!

Serves: 4
Prep Time: 20 minutes
Cook Time: 10 minutes

Ingredients:

- 2 tbsp. of unsalted butter
- 1 lb. of medium shrimp, shelled and deveined
- 2 cloves garlic, minced
- ½ tsp. of red pepper flakes

- ¼ cup of chicken stock
- Juice of 1 lemon
- 4 medium zucchini, spiralized
- 2 tbsp. of freshly grated Parmesan
- Chopped parsley, for garnish

Directions:

1. Preheat a large frying pan to medium temperature; melt the butter and fry, stirring constantly the flakes of garlic and red pepper for 1 minute.
2. Add shrimp. Cook for about 3 minutes.
3. Add chicken stock and lemon juice, and stir.
4. Add the zucchini noodles and cook, occasionally stirring, for 2 minutes.
5. Season with salt and pepper
6. Garnish with Parmesan and parsley.
7. Serve immediately.

Nutrients per serving:

- Calories: 162 kcal
- Fat: 7.45g
- Net Carbs: 4.91g
- Protein: 18.14g

10. Baked Cauliflower with Cheese

The preparation of the dish is straightforward. It requires a small amount of ingredients and, most importantly, it is prepared very quickly!

You can use cauliflower in large quantities without being afraid of gaining weight. This valuable diet product also has a unique taste. Cauliflower can be used both fresh and frozen.

Servings: 4
Prep Time: 15 minutes
Cook Time: 35 minutes

Ingredients:
- 1 head of cauliflower, cut into florets
- 1 cup of heavy cream
- Sliced bacon, cooked
- 1/2 cup of shredded cheddar cheese
- ¼ cup of chopped green onions
- 2 oz. of cream cheese
- 2 tbsps. of butter
- Salt and pepper

Directions:
1. Preheat your oven to 350°F.
2. Boil water, and cook your florets for 2 minutes. Drain them after.
3. In a pot, melt the butter, heavy cream, cream cheese, half of the cheddar cheese and season it after being thoroughly combined.
4. In a baking dish, mix everything; all except a bit of bacon, green onions, and the rest of the cheddar.
5. Use those to top your meal.
6. Bake until golden; around 25-30 minutes.

Nutrients per serving:
- Calories: 498 kcal
- Fat: 45 g
- Carbs: 6 g
- Protein: 14 g

Chapter 3 – Dinner

1. Rissole in Bacon

What do you cook with minced meat? There is one beautiful, simple, and easy recipe. I will tell you how to prepare the chops in bacon. Such rissole is cooked easily and quickly!

Serves: 4
Prep Time: 15 minutes
Cook Time: 30 minutes

Ingredients:
- 1 lb. of ground beef
- 2 oz. of cheddar cheese
- 20 bacon slices

- 4 tbsp. of peanut butter
- 1 tsp. of garlic powder
- 1 tsp. of onion powder
- 1 tsp. of salt
- ½ tsp. of pepper

Directions:
1. Mix the ground beef and seasonings.
2. Divide the meat and form them into four patties with your hands.
3. Cook on the grill until done.
4. Add 1 tablespoon peanut butter and sprinkle cheese onto each cooked burger.
5. Wrap up your burger in the bacon. About 5 slice per patty.
6. Cook for about 20 minutes in the oven at 400°F or 200°C until the bacon begins to brown or when it has reached your preferred texture.
7. Serve with lettuce, red onion, or any desired toppings.

Nutrition Facts per Serving:
- Calories: 850 kcal
- Fat: 67.8g
- Carbs: 8.13g
- Protein: 49.82g

2. Stuffed Chicken Peppers

Well and deliciously stuffed peppers. The stuffing is not done the way it is usually done with stuffed peppers. It has chicken, Greek yogurt and avocado.

Servings: 3

Prep Time: 5 minutes

Cook Time: 40 minutes

Ingredients:
- 3 peppers cut in half, and the seeds and membranes removed
- 200 g boiled chicken breast cut into cubes
- 1 small white onion, chopped finely

- 1 avocado, cut into cubes
- 1 garlic clove (optional), chopped finely
- 1 tablespoon lime juice
- 140 g Greek yogurt
- 1 hot pepper, chopped finely
- 25 g fresh cilantro, chopped finely
- Salt, black and red pepper to taste

Directions:
1. Preheat oven to 360° F degrees.
2. Blanch the halves of the peppers in low-boiling salted water for 3 minutes.
3. Mix all other ingredients for mince.
4. Fill the halves of the peppers with stuffing.
5. Put the peppers in the form and put them in the oven.
6. Bake for 20-25 minutes.

Enjoy!

Nutrients per serving:
- Calories: 110.91 kcal
- Carbs: 60.5 g
- Fats: 5.3 g
- Protein: 9.40 g

3. Egg Keto Salad with Avocado

I offer you a recipe for an original dinner of avocado and eggs. The dish has an interesting taste; it is delicate and silky in texture; and due to the mustard, it is not devoid of spicy sharpness. Great for dinner!

Servings: 1
Prep Time: 5 minutes
Cook Time: 10 minutes

Ingredients:

- 1 Avocado
- 2 Eggs

- 0.5 lemon (2 tbsp).
- Olive oil 20 g
- Mustard salt and pepper.

Directions:

1. Boil eggs and separate the whites from the yolks. Squirrel cut into cubes.
2. Finely chop the avocado.
3. Prepare the sauce: knead the yolks with a fork in a deep plate and add lemon, mustard, oil, salt, and pepper. Stir until smooth. It is possible in a blender.
4. Mix egg whites, avocado, and sauce.
5. This salad goes well with keto pancakes.

Nutrients per serving:

- Calories: 210 kcal
- Fat: 18.25 g
- Carbs: 5.56 g
- Protein: 5.62 g

4. Baked Eggs with Ham and Asparagus

Try this dish; it looks great and will surprise you with its taste!

Servings: 2
Prepare Time: 5 minutes
Cook Time: 15 minutes

Ingredients:

- 6 eggs
- 6 slices (about 100 g) of Italian ham
- 226 g of asparagus
- A few sprigs of fresh marjoram
- 1 tbsp. of butter or ghee

Directions:

1. In a baking sheet with a muffin pan, put the ham down and around the hole so as to close the bottom and sides.
2. Add a few twigs of marjoram.
3. Pour 1 egg into each form.
4. Bake in the oven for 10 - 12 minutes at 180 degrees.
5. Steam the asparagus, and then season it with butter.
6. Put all the ingredients on a plate and enjoy.

Nutrients per serving:

- Calories: 424.6 kcal
- Fat: 31.5 g
- Carbs: 3.7 g
- Protein: 33.5 g

5. Egg Keto Pizza

This pizza recipe is very simple and easy to make! The carbohydrate-free pizza dough turns out incredibly tasty, and just fantastic! Stuffing can add to your favorite from keto-friendly products.

Servings: 2
Prepare Time: 5 minutes
Cook Time: 20 minutes

Ingredients:

Dough:
- 2 cups of grated cauliflower

- 2 tbsp. of coconut flour
- 1/2 tsp. of salt
- 4 eggs
- 1 tbsp. of psyllium powder
- Filling: To your taste - it can be smoked salmon, avocado, greens, spinach, olive oil, bacon, eggs, chimichurri sauce, or fried vegetables.

Directions:

1. Mix the ingredients for the dough, and then set it aside for 5 minutes.
2. Pour the dough into the pan and smooth it out.
3. Bake for 15 minutes.
4. Remove from the oven, and then place the top of your choice on top.

Nutrients per serving:

- Calories: 454 kcal
- Fat: 31 g
- Carbs: 6.1 g
- Protein: 22 g

6. Egg Rolls

Want to make something new and unusual for dinner? Then try the egg roll. This breakfast can be eaten every day; changing the filling - it will always be individually and tasty! Moreover, it is easy to cook this egg dish, and the set of products is selected to taste.

Servings: 5
Prepare Time: 5 minutes
Cook Time: 20 minutes

Ingredients:

- 10 large eggs
- Salt and pepper to taste

- 1.5 cups of shredded cheddar cheese
- 5 slices of bacon

Directions:

1. Whisk eggs, salt, pepper.
2. Fry in oil in a frying pan under the cover for about 5 minutes.
3. Pour about 1/3 cup of cheese on top.
4. Put a strip of bacon.
5. Carefully roll the egg into a roll and set aside a serving.
6. Repeat steps 1-3 to create 4 more rolls.

Nutrients per serving:

- Calories: 412 kcal
- Fat: 31.66 g
- Carbs: 2.26 g
- Protein: 28.21 g

7. Chicken Cutlets

Delicious, ruddy chicken mince patties are good anyway; you can take them with you to work or on the road - they are tasty even when cold.

Servings: 1
Prep Time: 5 minutes
Cook Time: 15minutes.

Ingredients:
- 200g-minced chicken
- 1 egg white
- 17g of oil
- Salt pepper to taste

Directions:

1. Whisk the egg white in thick foam.
2. Add the whipped egg white to the cooked minced meat, salt, and pepper to taste; mix gently.
3. Heat a thin layer of butter in a frying pan and fry until golden brown.

Nutrients per serving:

- Calories: 475 kcal
- Carbs: 0.8 g
- Fats: 36.16 g
- Protein: 37.35 g

8. Chicken Rolls with Parmesan

Chicken rolls - a great dish for dinner for two (including a festive one). The recipe is simple; the Directions time is minimal, which is always appreciated.

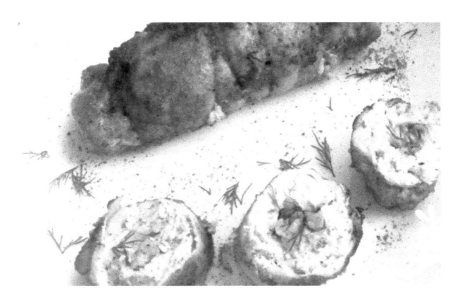

Servings: 3
Prep Time: 5 minutes
Cook Time: 20minutes

Ingredients:

- 60g of Parmesan cheese
- 3 pieces of Chicken Breast
- 2 tbsp. of Almond flour

- 2 tbsp. of Peanut Urbech
- 3-4 tbsp. of Olive/coconut oil. Salt and pepper to taste

Directions:

1. Grate the grated cheese, finely chop the nut.
2. Beat chicken breast fillets with a hammer into a thin layer.
3. In a bowl, mix urbech, cheese, and walnut. Put on the edge of the chicken breast and roll in the form of rolls.
4. Then roll finished rolls in almond flour.
5. And fry on all sides in a heated pan with the addition of oil.
6. Then you can cover and reduce the heat; leave for 5 minutes.
7. You can also cook these rolls, steamed or in the oven at 350 °F for about 7-10 minutes.

Nutrition :

- Calories: 645.66 kcal
- Fats: 35 g
- Carbs: 6.1 g
- Protein: 51.9 g

9. Turkey and Spinach Meatballs

Very tender and juicy; will just melt in your mouth. If you have never cooked them, then catch up.

Servings: 5
Prep Time: 5 minutes
Cook Time: 20minutes.

Ingredients:

- 730g of Turkey thigh fillet
- 1 Onion
- 45 g Egg

- 150g Spinach
- 20g Vegetable oil
- 1 tsp. of Sea salt
- 0.5 tsp. of ground black pepper

Directions:
1. Run the turkey fillet and onion through a meat grinder.
2. Add salt, pepper, egg, and spinach.
3. Mix everything until a homogeneous mass and form small balls.
4. Meatballs should be baked in a preheated 350 ° F oven for 15 minutes.

Nutrients per serving:
- Calories: 135.66 kcal
- Carbs: 3.8 g
- Fats: 11.2 g
- Protein: 32 g

10. Baked Chicken Fillet with Cheese

Soft and juicy chicken breast in the oven. The dish is very tasty; you can cook both on weekdays and for the festive table. This is a simple recipe for oven-baked chicken fillet.

Servings: 5
Prep Time: 10 minutes
Cook Time: 25minutes

Ingredients:

- 2 chicken fillets
- 1 Tablespoon of sour cream
- 30 grams of hard cheese
- Spice

Directions:

1. Divide the fillet into two parts along the fibers, and repulse well from both sides. Next, put it on a baking sheet.
2. Well, grease each piece of meat with sour cream (first mix sour cream with spices).
3. Put the meat in the oven for 20 minutes.
4. Next; get the fillet, and layout the cheese on it; bake until done.

Nutrients per serving:

- Calories: 600.66 kcal
- Carbs: 2.6 g
- Fats: 23.2 g
- Protein: 35.70 g

11. Turkey Rolls

Sometimes, to diversify your menu, it's enough to add a couple of new ingredients to a familiar dish. Very tasty, soft, and juicy are the rolls with zucchini.

Servings: 4
Prep Time: 5 minutes
Cook Time: 20minutes

Ingredients:

- 500 g of turkey meat
- 1pcs of avocado
- 1 piece of paprika

- 1pc of zucchini
- 2 tbsp. of Lemon juice
- 150 grams of cheese

Directions:

1. Bake the turkey meat.
2. Mash the cheese.
3. Combine avocados, pepper, and lemon juice; beat in a blender until smooth.
4. Cut the zucchini into small pieces.
5. Thinly chop the poultry meat and smear each slice with the resulting sauce.
6. Inside each slice, put a piece of zucchini and wrap.

Nutrients per serving:

- Calories: 386.6 kcal
- Carbs: 4.16 g
- Fats: 24.25 g
- Protein: 35.5 g

Chapter 4 - Fish Recipes

1. Monkfish Rolls with Ham

Delicate fish rolls with an unusual taste ... You can use this recipe as a separate dish or serve with a side dish.

Servings: 1
Prep Time: 5 minutes
Cook Time: 20 minutes

Ingredients:

- 2 cups of Lettuce leaves
- Salt and black pepper to taste
- ½ cup of Leek
- 1 tbsp. of Finely chopped parsley
- 1 Monkfish fillet

- 1 Ham
- 1 tbsp. of Olive oil

Directions:
1. Mix salt, pepper, shallot parsley, and olive oil.
2. Cut the monkfish fillet into 3 parts; add salt and pepper to taste.
3. A slice of ham (lengthwise); cut into 3 parts.
4. Wrap one piece of fish with one strip of ham, fix with a toothpick.
5. Fry the fish rolls on medium heat for about 3-4 minutes on each side.
6. Arrange the salad leaves on a plate, put the fish on top.
7. Pour dressing; serve.

A little tip:
Fish rolls do not need much time to get ready. Therefore, do not fry or simmer it for too long.

Nutrients per serving:
- Calories: 489.2 kcal
- Carbs: 4.41 g
- Fats: 43.15 g
- Protein: 49.25 g

2. Salmon Cutlets with Fresh Herbs

Delicate and juicy fish cakes with a matching side dish - a great dish for everyday and festive table.

Servings: 5
Prep Time: 5 minutes
Cook Time: 30 minutes

Ingredients:

- Canned salmon - 500g
- 25 g- Parmesan Cheese
- 120 g- chopped bacon
- 2 pcs. of Chicken Egg
- Salt and pepper greens to taste
- 100 ml of Almond flour

Directions:

1. Mix the salmon, parmesan cheese, chopped bacon, two large eggs, salt, and pepper.
2. Divide the minced meat by 10 patties.
3. Roll in the almond flour.
4. Fry the patties in olive oil until golden brown on each side.

Nutrients per serving:

- Calories: 435 kcal
- Carbs: 2.8 g
- Fats: 31.60 g
- Protein: 35.4 g

3. Salmon or Trout with Cream Sauce

Juicy, tender baked salmon, with dill sauce - an excellent treat.

Servings: 2

Prep Time: 5 minutes

Cook Time: 15 minutes

Ingredients

Sauce UKROPA

- 3/4 cup of sour cream
- 2 tsp. of Dijon mustard

- 1 garlic clove
- 2 1/2 tablespoons of fresh of dill
- 1 - 2 tablespoons of lemon juice
- 1/4 - 1/2 tsp. of salt

For the Fish:

- 1/2 - 1 tablespoon of butter
- 4 salmon or trout fillets (125 g / 4 oz. each)
- Salt and pepper

Directions:

1. Mix the ingredients for the sauce, and mix well.
2. Sprinkle the fish with salt and pepper.
3. Fry the fish in a pan of oil on both sides for 2 minutes.
4. Serve with dill sauce.

Nutrients per serving:

- Calories: 598 kcal
- Carbs: 1.5 g
- Fats: 51.25 g
- Protein: 50.07 g

4. Baked Shrimp with Garlic and Butter

A very popular dish in Greece - it is cooked simply and quickly, it turns out incredibly tasty!

Servings: 2
Prep Time: 5 minutes
Cook Time: 30 minutes

Ingredients:

- 1 pound of raw shrimp
- 5 tablespoons of softened butter
- 3-4 large cloves of garlic

- salt and freshly ground pepper

Directions:

1. Combine the shrimps with garlic salt, pepper, and butter.
2. Place them on a baking sheet, and bake for 10-15 minutes at 350º F

Nutrients per serving:

- Calories: 568 kcal
- Carbs: 0.5 g
- Fats: 43 g
- Protein: 48.9 g

5. Salmon Fruits with Sauce

I suggest Directions for meatballs from minced fish, in a creamy sauce. Fishballs for this recipe are appetizing, juicy and tasty; and are prepared simply.

Servings: 5
Prep Time: 5 minutes
Cook time: 30 minutes

Ingredients:
- 2 tablespoons of coconut oil
- 2 cloves of garlic
- 1 pound of ground salmon
- 1 big egg

For the lemon-cream sauce:

- 2 tablespoons of butter
- 1 medium lemon fruit juice and zest
- 2 tablespoons of Dijon mustard
- 2 cups of thick cream
- 2+ tablespoons of fresh green onions, chopped
- salt pepper to taste

Directions:

1. Mix salmon, garlic, and egg; add butter, and form meatballs.
2. Bake for 20-25 minutes in the oven at 200 degrees centigrade.
3. For the sauce, mix all the ingredients, and cook until it becomes thick.
4. Remove the cooked meatballs from the oven and place in the sauce.
5. Decorate with onions.

Nutrients per serving:
- Calories: 380 kcal
- Carbs: 5 g
- Fats: 31 g
- Protein: 20 g

6. Fried Salmon with Parmesan

Salmon is tasty in itself, so for its preparation, it is necessary to add quite a bit of herb and spices. A simple recipe for grilled salmon will allow you to save the wonderful natural taste of fresh fish.

Servings: 2
Prep Time: 5 minutes
Cook Time: 12 minutes

Ingredients:
- 2 pieces of salmon (only about 1.5 kg)
- ¼ cup of mayonnaise
- ¼ cup of grated parmesan cheese
- 1 tablespoon of ground dill

- 1 teaspoon of ground mustard

Directions:

1. Add the mayo in a bowl that can fit the salmon pieces.
2. In another bowl, combine the dill, mustard, and parmesan.
3. Coat each salmon piece in the mayo, and then in the parmesan mix.
4. Fry over medium heat for 4 minutes per side.
5. Serve and Enjoy!

Nutrients per serving:

- Calories: 550 kcal
- Carbs: 6 g
- Fats: 38 g
- Protein: 48 g

7. Salmon with Seasoning

Delicious, the delicate fish, and very healthy Salmon, cooked in all its beauty and taste. Preparing it is very easy. Salmon has a lot of Omega-3, which is so necessary for our heart.

Servings: 2
Prep Time: 5 minutes
Cook Time: 15minutes

Ingredients:

- 2 teaspoons of coconut oil
- 1 ½ teaspoon of salt
- 1 teaspoon of Italian seasonings
- ½ teaspoon of crushed red pepper

- ¼ teaspoon of ground black pepper
- 1 ½ pounds of boneless salmon filet, skin removed
- 1 avocado
- ¼ cup of chopped basil
- 1 tablespoon of lime juice

Directions:

1. Turn on medium-high heat and heat the oil in a cast-iron skillet.
2. Sprinkle ¾ teaspoon salt, Italian seasonings, crushed red pepper and black pepper over the salmon, and coat well.
3. Lay salmon fillet, with the skinned side up, in the hot oil. Let it cook undisturbed until lightly browned and perfectly crispy along the bottom edge. Cook until the flesh is cooked about halfway up the side of the filet for 4 to 6 minutes.
4. Flip the fish over and remove the skillet from the heat. Allow the fish to remain in the hot skillet, so that the heat can be carried over to continue with Directions at the other side until the desired doneness is attained in another 4 minutes.
5. The next step is to peel, remove the pit, and mash the avocado.
6. Add basil, lime juice and a ¾ teaspoon of salt.

7. Serve salmon topped with avocado mash. If desired, you can sprinkle it with scallions.

Nutrition

- Calories: 232kcal
- Fat: 4g
- Carbs: 7g
- Protein: 32g

Chapter 5 - Snacks / Salads

1. Cheese Keto Chips

Homemade cheese chips - a new taste of the famous dish! Cook quickly, eat deliciously!

Servings: 2

Prep Time: 5 minutes

Cook Time: 15 minutes

Ingredients:

- 1 ½ cups shredded cheddar cheese
- 3 tablespoons of flax flour

- Seasonings of your choice

Directions:

1. Sprinkle a handful of cheddar cheese on a non-stick baking sheet, and sprinkle with a pinch of flax flour.
2. Add seasonings to your taste and bake for 10 minutes at 350 F degrees.
3. Optional: during baking, you can put bacon slices on top.

Nutrients per serving:

- Calories: 65.83 kcal
- Carbs: 0.56 g
- Fats: 5.72 g
- Protein: 3.61 g

2. Spicy Eggs

This recipe is delicious, beautiful, and very effective! Watch and cook with us!

Servings: 3
Prep Time: 5 minutes
Cook Time: 15 minutes

Ingredients

- 4 eggs
- 3 ounces of finely grated parmesan cheese
- 2 ounces of heavy whipped cream (1/4 cup)
- 1/2 oz. of Fresh spinach finely chopped
- salt pepper to taste

Directions:

1. Using a silicone egg mold, spread the spinach evenly across the forms.
2. In a bowl, mix the eggs, parmesan cheese, cream, salt, and pepper. Beat until smooth.
3. Pour the mixture into the molds.
4. Bake in the oven at 350 F, for 10 minutes.

Nutrients per serving:

- Calories: 359 kcal
- Carbs: 2.5 g
- Fats: 29 g
- Protein: 27 g

3. Eggs with Spices

Very tasty and classic recipe. The snack will be appetizing and unusual!

Servings: 6
Prep Time: 5 minutes
Cook Time: 20 minutes

Ingredients:
- 6 eggs
- 1/4 cup of mayonnaise
- 1 teaspoon of Dijon mustard
- salt and pepper to taste

For Filling:
- 1/8 teaspoon of paprika

- 1 tablespoon of chopped fresh green onions
- 1 piece of cooked bacon crumbles

Directions:
1. Boil eggs for 6 minutes; slice each egg lengthwise.
2. Scrape egg yolks in a large bowl and mash them.
3. Add mayonnaise, mustard, salt, and pepper. Mix until smooth.
4. Place the egg yolk mixture in a small plastic sandwich bag.
5. Cut a tiny corner and pour it over each egg. Garnish with paprika, fresh onions and bacon crumbs.

Nutrients per serving:
- Calories: 160 kcal
- Carbs: 0.5 g
- Fats: 13 g
- Protein: 6 g

4. Egg Keto-Cupcakes

Bright and tasty snack cupcakes on eggs.

Servings: 6

Prep Time: 5 minutes

Cook Time: 30 minutes

Ingredients:

- 12 eggs
- 226 g of ground beef
- 1/4 cup of 36% heavy cream
- 1/2 tsp. of garlic powder
- A pinch of salt

Directions:

1. Fry ground beef until fully cooked.
2. Mix eggs with cream and minced meat. Add garlic powder, salt, and spices to taste.
3. Spread the mixture into oiled forms. Bake for 25 minutes at 350 degrees F.

Nutrients per serving:

- Calories: 147 kcal
- Carbs: 1.5 g
- Fats: 11 g
- Protein: 10 g

5. Kale Chips

That you have not tried! Kale leaf chips - a very refreshing homemade snack, which is not difficult to cook. If you want to please yourself and loved ones with excellent chips, prepare this recipe!

Serves: 2

Prep Time: 10 minutes

Cook Time: 5 minutes

Ingredients:

- 3 tsp. of olive oil
- 12 pieces of kale leaves
- Salt and pepper, as needed

Directions:

1. Preheat oven to 350°F.
2. Line a baking sheet with parchment paper.
3. Wash and thoroughly dry kale leave and place them on the baking sheet.
4. Smear kale with olive oil and sprinkle with salt and pepper.
5. Bake 10 to 15 minutes.
6. Serve.

Nutrition Facts per Serving:

- Calories: 107 kcal
- Carbs: 8.4g
- Carbs: 4.9g
- Protein: 4.11g

6. Peanut Butter Cookie

Want to make elementary, tasty, and incredibly aromatic peanut cookies at home? Then hurry to remember this fantastic recipe for this snack and repeat it in your kitchen.

Serves: 12
Prep Time: 15 minutes
Cook Time: 10 minutes

Ingredients:

- 1 cup of peanut butter
- ½ cup of powdered erythritol
- 1 egg

Directions:

1. Preheat oven to 350°F.
2. In a medium bowl, combine the peanut butter, erythritol, and the egg. Mix well.
3. Form the cookie dough into 1-inch balls.
4. Place the balls on a parchment paper-lined baking sheet.
5. Press down on the dough with a fork twice, in opposite directions. Repeat with the rest of the dough.
6. Bake for about 13 minutes.
7. Let cool for 5 minutes before serving.

Nutrients per serving:

- Calories: 80 kcal
- Fat: 9.12g
- Carbs: 5.96g
- Protein: 2.91g

7. Cheesy Cauliflower Croquettes

Cauliflower croquettes are beautiful whether hot or cold. Excellent. They go under different sauces - sharp, sweet, sour. Be sure to try the Directions of cauliflower croquettes for a snack.

Servings: 4
Prep Time: 10 minutes
Cook Time: 30 minutes

Ingredients:
- 2 cups of cauliflower florets
- 2 tsps. of minced garlic
- ½ cups of chopped onion
- ½ tsp. of salt

- ½ tsp. of pepper
- 2 tbsps. of butter
- ¾ cups of grated cheddar cheese

Directions:
1. Place butter in a microwave-safe bowl; then melts the butter. Let it cool.
2. Place cauliflower florets in a food processor; then process until smooth and becoming crumbles.
3. Transfer the cauliflower crumbles to a bowl and then add chopped onion and cheese.
4. Season with minced garlic, salt, and pepper. Pour melted butter over the mixture.
5. Shape the cauliflower mixture into medium balls and arrange in the Air Fryer.
6. Preheat an Air Fryer to 400°F and cook the cauliflower croquettes for 14 minutes.
7. To achieve a more golden brown color, cook the cauliflower croquettes for another 2 minutes.

Nutritional:
- Calories: 160 kcal
- Fat: 13g
- Protein: 6.8g
- Carbs: 5.1g

Chapter 6: Ketogenic Sauces

1. Keto Parmesan Pesto

We strongly recommend that you learn how to make a homemade "Pesto" sauce - an incredibly creamy egg sauce with a bright, refreshing taste that is suitable for chips, snacks, and salads!

Serves: 6 (about two tablespoons)
Prep Time: 5 minutes
Total Time: 5 minutes

Ingredients:

- 1 Cup Full of Fat Cream Cheese
- 2 Tablespoons of Basil Pesto
- ½ Cup of Parmesan Cheese, Grated
- 8 Olives, Sliced
- Salt and Pepper to Taste

Directions:

1. Mix all of your ingredients in a mixing bowl.
2. Refrigerate for at least 20 minutes before serving.

Nutrients per serving:

- Calories: 161 kcal
- Fat: 14.33 g
- Carbs: 3.23 g
- Protein: 5.42 g

2. Salsa Sauce

The high-quality sauce can significantly improve the taste of the dish, as well as give unusual flavors. This is especially true for spicy additives. They are often used in recipes of Mexican cuisine.

Prepare Time: 5 minutes

Ingredients:

- 3 tbsps. of cider vinegar
- 4 tbsps. of olive oil
- 2 tbsps. of sour cream
- 2 tbsps. of mayo

- 1 tsp. of chili powder
- 1 garlic clove
- ½ cup of salsa sauce

Directions:

1. Whisk all ingredients in the bowl until smooth. Or you can shake them all together in a tight-fitting jar.
2. Season it to your taste. You can dilute it with water if you want a thinner sauce.

Nutrients per serving:

- Carbs: 2 g
- Fat: 21 g
- Protein: 1 g
- Calories: 200 kcal

3. Blue Cheese Sauce

From a few simple ingredients in just 5 minutes, you can make a fresh sauce. It will complement the pizza, sandwiches, vegetables, as well as zucchini pasta, and favorite snacks. Great recipe!

Prepare Time: 5 minutes

Ingredients:

- ¾ cup of Greek yogurt
- 5 oz. of bleu cheese
- ½ cup of mayo
- Heavy whipping cream

- 2 tbsps. of fresh parsley
- Salt and pepper

Directions:

1. Break the cheese into chunks in a small bowl, and then add yogurt and mayo before mixing well.
2. Let it sit for a few minutes.
3. Dilute in water or heavy cream for your desired consistency and season with greens, salt, and pepper.

Nutrients per serving:

- Carbs: 3 g
- Fat: 36 g
- Protein: 9 g
- Calories: 375 kcal

4. Thai Peanut Sauce

I recommend peanut butter sauce to lovers of all original and new recipes. With it, any meat dish or a simple chicken will play with new colors! Watch and write!

Prepare Time: 8 minutes

Ingredients:

- ½ ounce of ginger root
- ½ tbsp. of garlic
- ¼ tsp. of molasses
- ½ cup of peanut butter
- 1 tbsp. of Stevia
- 1 tbsp. of sesame oil

- 3 tbsps. of chicken broth
- 3 tbsps. of soy sauce
- 3 tbsps. of hot sauce
- 2 tbsps. of lime juice

Directions:

1. Mix all ingredients smoothly.
2. Place it in a jar and cover it.
3. Leave it for at least a night before using, and store it in the refrigerator.

Nutrients per serving:

- Calories: 158 kcal
- Fat: 13 g
- Protein: 6 g
- Carbs: 3 g

5. Avocado & Yogurt Sauce with Salad Cilantro

This sauce is excellent for salad dressing. You can also try it with meat. The main ingredients of the sauce are perfectly combined. Lime gives a few citrus notes, and garlic and pepper make it spicier.

It is prepared very quickly because all the ingredients are mixed in a grinder.

Prepare Time: 15 minutes

Ingredients:

- 1 avocado
- 2 tablespoons of cilantro

- 1 garlic clove
- 1 tablespoon of lime juice
- 1/4 teaspoon of black pepper
- 1/4 of teaspoon salt
- 3 tablespoons of olive oil
- 100 g Greek yogurt

Directions:

1. Put the ingredients in the chopper bowl and chop to the desired consistency.

You can fill them with salad.

Nutrients per serving:

- Carbs: 381 g
- Fat: 11.72 g
- Protein: 2.1 g
- Calories: 123 kcal

Chapter 7 – Keto Approved Desserts

1. Chocolate Pancakes

Delicious dessert idea; tender, aromatic, soft and fluffy pancakes are perfectly combined with whipped cream.

Servings: 8
Prep Time: 5 minutes
Cook Time: 20minutes

Ingredients:

- 1 1/2 cups of almond flour

- 1 tbsp. of keto-friendly sweetener of your choice
- 1 tsp. of baking powder
- 2 eggs
- 2 tbsp. of coconut oil
- 3 tbsp. (tablespoons) of chopped dark chocolate without sugar

Directions:

1. Put all ingredients (except chocolate) in a large bowl and mix.
2. Leave the dough for 3-5 minutes.
3. Add chopped chocolate.
4. Fry the pancakes for 3-4 minutes on each side, in coconut oil.
5. Serve with berries or fatty whipped cream.

Nutrients per serving:

- Calories: 123 kcal
- Carbs: 2 g
- Fats: 15 g
- Protein: 10 g

2. Chocolate Brownie in a Mug

It is very easy to prepare. You can do it at once for one person and the oven should not be used at all. This recipe is prepared in the microwave.

Servings: 10
Prep Time: 5 minutes
Cook Time: 20minutes

Ingredients:

- 1 Large egg
- 2 tbsp. of almond flour
- 1/2 tsp. of baking powder

- 2 tbsp. of unsweetened cocoa powder
- 1 tbsp. of butter or coconut oil, or ghee
- 1/2 tsp. of vanilla extract
- 1 tbsp. of stevia or keto-friendly sweetener of your choice

Directions:

1. Grease the mugs that you will use to make the brownies.
2. Stir all ingredients with a whisk until smooth.
3. Pour the dough into the prepared form, and put inside the microwave for about 1 minute (two servings) or 75 seconds per serving.

Nutrients per serving:

- Calories: 140 kcal
- Fats: 9 g
- Carbs: 3 g
- Protein: 11 g

3. Chocolate Truffles

Chocolate truffles are what you need if you like chocolate. Easy to prepare, and the effect is stunning. Real chocolate natural candies made by your own hands. It is like it is in France, but without sugar.

Servings: 15
Prep Time: 5 minutes
Cook Time: 15minutes

Ingredients:

- 2 avocados
- 50 g of melted cocoa butter
- 24 g of melted coconut oil

- 30 g of cocoa chocolate
- Stevia or other keto sweetener of your choice
- Optional: topping of your choice - chopped nuts, cocoa powder, chia seeds, etc. The sprinkling is not included in the macros below, so be sure to adjust them!

Directions:

1. Mix all the ingredients. Beat with a blender until no lumps remain in the mixture.
2. Refrigerate for at least 2 hours.
3. Divide the mixture into 15 equal parts and form balls.
4. Sprinkle with sprinkling to your taste.

Nutrition :

- Calories: 235 kcal
- Fats: 8 g
- Carbs: 1 g
- Protein: 1 g

4. Chia Pudding

Nutritionists call chia seeds a "superfood" because it contains many minerals, vitamins, antioxidants, and fiber. Regular consumption of this product contributes to weight loss - chia stimulates the functions that are involved in burning fat.

Servings: 1
Prep Time: 5 minutes
Cook Time: 30minutes

Ingredients:

- 100 g of fatty coconut milk
- 15 g of chia seeds
- 0.5 g of stevia
- 0.2 g of ground cinnamon

Directions:

1. Mix all ingredients well together. The mixture will be very liquid.
2. Leave for 30 minutes. Chia seeds should swell and soften, so that the pudding can have a much thicker consistency. If necessary, dilute with water.

Nutrition :

- Calories: 228 kcal
- Fats: 19 g
- Carbs: 6 g
- Protein: 4.28 g

5. Chocolate Keto Cake with Blueberry

This is an ordinary cake that is very tasty, and will appeal even to those who do not eat according to the keto-diet. My son, who is skeptical of any keto desserts, tried it and approved it. So go for it!

In it, of course, there is cottage cheese. But use the fattest curd. All together - this is a real fat bomb! It's nutrient profile is very keto.

Servings: 8
Prepare Time: 10 minutes
Cook Time: 40 minutes

Ingredients:

- 2 eggs, stripped into whites and yolks
- 25 g of cocoa powder
- 50 g of almond flour
- 20 g of flax flour
- 1 tsp. of sweetener (or to taste)
- 150 g of sour cream
- 50 g of vegetable oil
- 2 tsp. of baking powder
- Vanilla or vanilla extract to taste

Directions:

1. Turn on the oven to 350 F degrees.
2. Beat the squirrel to stable foam.
3. Beat yolks with sweetener.
4. Add sour cream and vegetable oil and mix.
5. Add all the dry ingredients and mix again, you can use a mixer.
6. Add proteins in two steps and mix them gently into the dough.
7. Use the form 16 cm in diameter.
8. Put in the oven for 25 minutes.
9. Cut the cake into two. You can soak them with a mixture of 1 tbsp. of water and 1 tsp. of Liquor.

10. For the cream, beat all ingredients with a mixer.

11. Spread the cake and put the cake in the fridge to soak over the night.

Nutrients per serving:
- Calories: 295.50 kcal
- Fat: 27.65 g
- Carbs: 7.94 g
- Protein: 7.25 g

6. Chocolate Mousse

Chocolate mousse is an exquisite delicacy that can be served at a party as a dessert; make an airy layer of chocolate cake. Help yourself!

Servings: 4
Prepare Time: 5 minutes
Cook Time: 5 minutes

Ingredients:

- 1 tbsp. of cocoa powder
- 2 oz. of cream cheese
- 2 oz. of butter

- 3 oz. of heavy whipping cream
- Stevia to taste

Directions:

1. Melt the butter a bit and mix with the sweetener. Stir until blended.
2. Add the cream cheese and cocoa powder and blend until smooth.
3. Carefully whip heavy cream and gradually add to the mixture.
4. Refrigerate it for 30 minutes

Nutrients per serving:

- Calories: 227 kcal
- Fat: 24 g
- Carbs: 3 g
- Protein: 4 g

7. Delicious Brownies

Diet is not a reason to deny yourself of the pleasure of indulging in sweets. You only need to choose the right sweets. For example, cook a low-carb brownie.

Servings: 4
Prep Time: 10 minutes
Cook Time: 25 minutes

Ingredients:

- 5 ounces of chocolate 86% (sugarless); melted
- 4 tablespoons of ghee, melted
- 3 eggs
- ½ cup of Swerve

- ¼ cup of mascarpone cheese
- ¼ cup of cocoa powder

Directions:

1. Take a big bowl; combine the melted chocolate with the ghee, eggs, swerve, cheese and cocoa. Whisk well, pour into a cake pan, introduce in the oven and cook at 375 degrees F for 25 minutes.
2. Cut into medium brownies and serve.

Nutrients per serving:

- Calories 120 kcal
- Fat: 8 g
- Carbs: 3 g
- Protein: 3 g

8. Coconut Raspberry Cake

Sweet tooth, attention! Today I want to share with you just a fantastic recipe for coconut cake; very gentle and melting in your mouth! Be sure to prepare it for the next holiday!

Servings: 6

Preparation Time: 1 hour and 10 minutes

Cook Time: 10 Minutes

Ingredients:

For the biscuit:

- 2 cups almond flour
- 1 egg
- 1 tablespoon of ghee, melted
- ½ teaspoon of baking soda

- For the coconut layer:
- 1 cup of coconut milk
- ¼ cup of coconut oil, melted
- 3 cups coconut, shredded
- 1/3 cup of stevia
- 5 grams of food gelatin

For the raspberry layer:
- 1 cup of raspberries
- 1 teaspoon of stevia
- 3 tablespoons of chia seeds
- 5 grams of food gelatin

Directions:

1. In a bowl, combine the almond flour with the eggs, ghee and baking soda; stir well. Press on the bottom of the spring form pan, and introduce in the oven at 350 degrees F for 15 minutes. Leave aside to cool down.
2. Meanwhile, in a pan, combine the raspberries with 1-teaspoon stevia, chia seeds, and gelatin; stir, and cook for 5 minutes. Take off the heat, cool down and spread over the biscuit layer.
3. In another small pan, combine the coconut milk with the coconut, oil, gelatin, 1/3 cup stevia; stir for 1-2 minutes.

Take off the heat, cool down and spread over the coconut milk.

4. Cool the cake in the fridge for 1 hour, slice and serve.

Nutrients per serving:
- Calories: 241 kcal
- Fat: 12 g
- Carbs: 5 g
- Protein: 5 g

9. Ice Cream with Avocado

Do you like ice cream? Today, I will tell you how to make a tasty and straightforward avocado ice cream at home! Everything is straightforward and fast; even no special equipment is needed!

Servings: 6
Prep Time: 10 minutes
Cook Time: 30 minutes

Ingredients:

- 1 peeled and pitted the avocado
- 1½ tsp. of vanilla paste
- 1 c.cm. of coconut milk

- 2 tbsps. of almond butter
- Drops of stevia
- ¼ tsp. of Ceylon cinnamon

Directions:

1. Combine all ingredients in a food blender.
2. Blend until smooth.
3. Transfer the mixture into Popsicle molds and insert Popsicle sticks.
4. Freeze for 4 hours or until firm.
5. Serve.

Nutrients per serving:

- Calories: 41 kcal
- Fats: 10 g
- Net Carbs 0.1 g
- Protein 0 g

Conclusion

Thanks for taking a culinary adventure in this book.

Make sure you eat consciously. In this way, you will enjoy every bite and will always cherish every meal that you prepare and eat.

We am sure you will see great results with the above recipes and meal plan. Remember that nutritional value is calculated per serving. To make things easier, that is, to cook less and not to throw out leftovers in terms of nutrition, I added leftovers as part of the meal.

How about replacing the ingredient? Yes you can. But you will need to recalculate macros for the recipe. First, you will need to find the nutrients for each ingredient. Then divide them by the number of servings that the recipe gives, and you will get the values for 1 serving.

Well, now it's time to start a diet and no longer renew it. Think of the huge benefits that you will get besides losing weight. Keto was created to enjoy this type of life, so you won't even notice when it actually becomes your lifestyle.

Kitchen Conversions

Weight conversions

METRIC	CUPS	OUNCES
15 g	1 tablespoon	1/2 ounce
30 g	1/8 cup	1 ounce
60 g	1/4 cup	2 ounces
115 g	1/2 cup	4 ounces
170 g	3/4 cup	6 ounces
225 g	1 cup	8 ounces
450 g	2 cups	16 ounces

Oven temperatures

CELSIUS	FAHRENHEIT
95°C	200°F
130°C	250°F
150°C	300°F
160°C	325°F
175°C	350°F
190°C	375°F
200°C	400°F
230°C	450°F

Length

METRIC	IMPERIAL
3 mm	1/8 inch
6 mm	1/4 inch
2.5 cm	1 inch
3 cm	1 1/4 inch
5 cm	2 inches
10 cm	4 inches
15 cm	6 inches
20 cm	8 inches
22.5 cm	9 inches
25 cm	10 inches
28 cm	11 inches

Volume conversions

METRIC	CUPS	OUNCES
15 ml	1 tablespoon	1/2 fl. oz
30 ml	2 tablespoons	1 fl. oz
60 ml	1/4 cup	2 fl. oz
125 ml	1/2 cup	4 fl. oz
180 ml	3/4 cup	6 fl. oz
250 ml	1 cup	8 fl. oz
500 ml	2 cups	16 fl. oz
1000 ml	4 cups	1 quart

CPSIA information can be obtained
at www.ICGtesting.com
Printed in the USA
LVHW081935221119
638070LV00014B/1265/P